DEAD
OF
WINTER

A collection
of photographs
taken in winter

Photography by Circe Denyer

Dead of Winter

All images are copyrighted © 2015 Circe Denyer.
http://publicdomainphotographs.com
ISBN 13: 978-1511986632
ISBN 10: 1511986638

Dead of Winter

Circe Denyer, 2015

Dead of winter in 2013
You met me at my discontent
Then, helped me understand your character

I, coddled in the warmth
Of manufactured heat
Viewed your beauty
And could not help but be drawn to you

Once it was evident
You would not harm my bones
I could join you
Enjoy you

Then see your difference
Your delicate difference

You came quietly
Quickly
Splenderously

Covering every inch with
White

I knew the wet
From winters past
I knew the wind
Every year it came unannounced

The white, I did not know
Not well
Not intimately
I avoided your frozen
Harsh and painful ways

I had tried once to know you
And failed with an ill feeling
Dead of Winter, I did not want you
I had not cared to meet

I did not know you
Until you invited me
With your crystals
and your powder

In the dead of winter
I found joy in the cold
I found happiness in the white
I was reborn that dead of winter

"I prefer winter and fall when you feel the bone structure of the landscape — the loneliness of it — the dead feeling of winter."

– Andrew Wyeth

Acknowledgements

The photographs in this book would not be here had I not been introduced to photography in Junior High School. It was my mother that stood in line at the school district to secure me a transfer from the school I should have attended to the one that had photography classes. I knew nothing about cameras, lenses, depth of field or processing film. I took six semesters in Junior High School and six in High School.

I am grateful for her desire to see me attend a school in an area she felt was better for me. I am grateful there was a photography program to expand my knowledge for the future.

These photographs would not have been taken had my dear friend Linnaea not introduced me to the wonders of winter. She has a sense of adventure and I grew from the experiences. I attribute the images of winter to her, for it was her invitation that took me to meet snow on a level I had not previously known.

I am grateful for stock photography sales sites that beckon me to create better and share the images from my camera.

I am appreciative to Law of Attraction for attracting beautiful things to my experience; always when I have my camera in-hand.

Foreword

Dead of Winter came to me as I photographed my least favorite season. It turned into my favorite when I discovered the reflection that the winter water makes. Snow, rain, and the aftermath of either are perfect subjects for a photographer looking for something new.
Each droplet of rain or crystal of snow has a unique reflection and shape.

The book contains quotes, poems and photographs from winter subjects.
Let the book find a place in your experience the way winter did in mine.

"Beauty can be seen in all things, seeing and composing the beauty is what separates the snapshot from the photograph.
– Matt Hardy

No one can look at a pine tree in winter without knowing that Spring will come again in due time.
                    -Frank Bolles

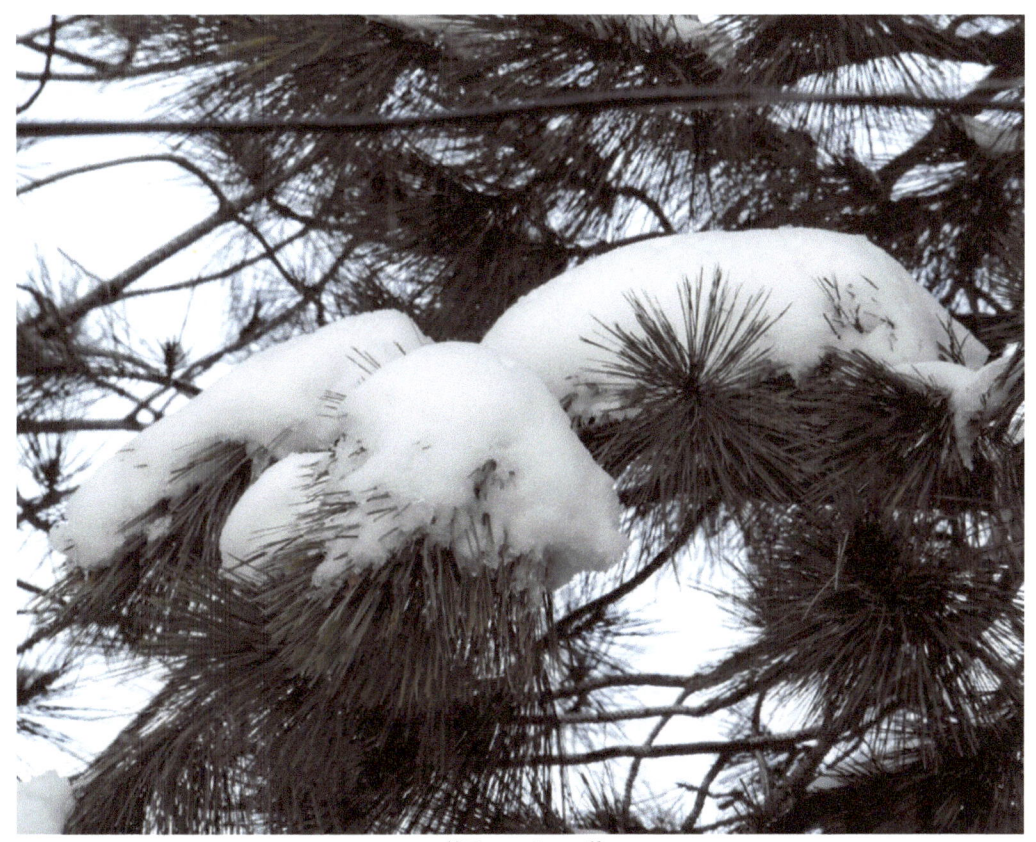

"Resting"

When Snow Falls

Not like the rain that patters
Not like the wind that howls
Snow falls quietly from the sky above
Quietly
Without a sound
Snow falls quietly from the clouds overhead
Then sits
Drifts
Covers
Then waits for you to notice it has changed the day to white.

-Circe Denyer, 2015

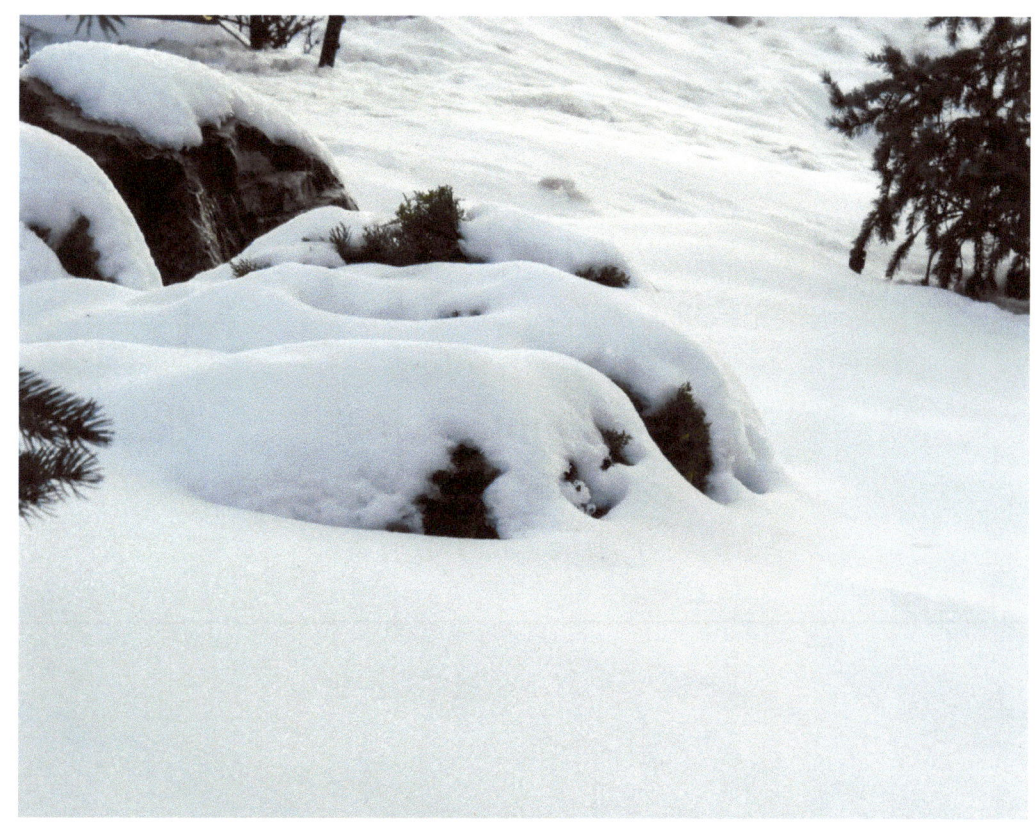

"When Snow Falls"

In a way winter
is the real spring —
the time when
the inner things happen,
the resurgence of nature.
-Edna O'Brien

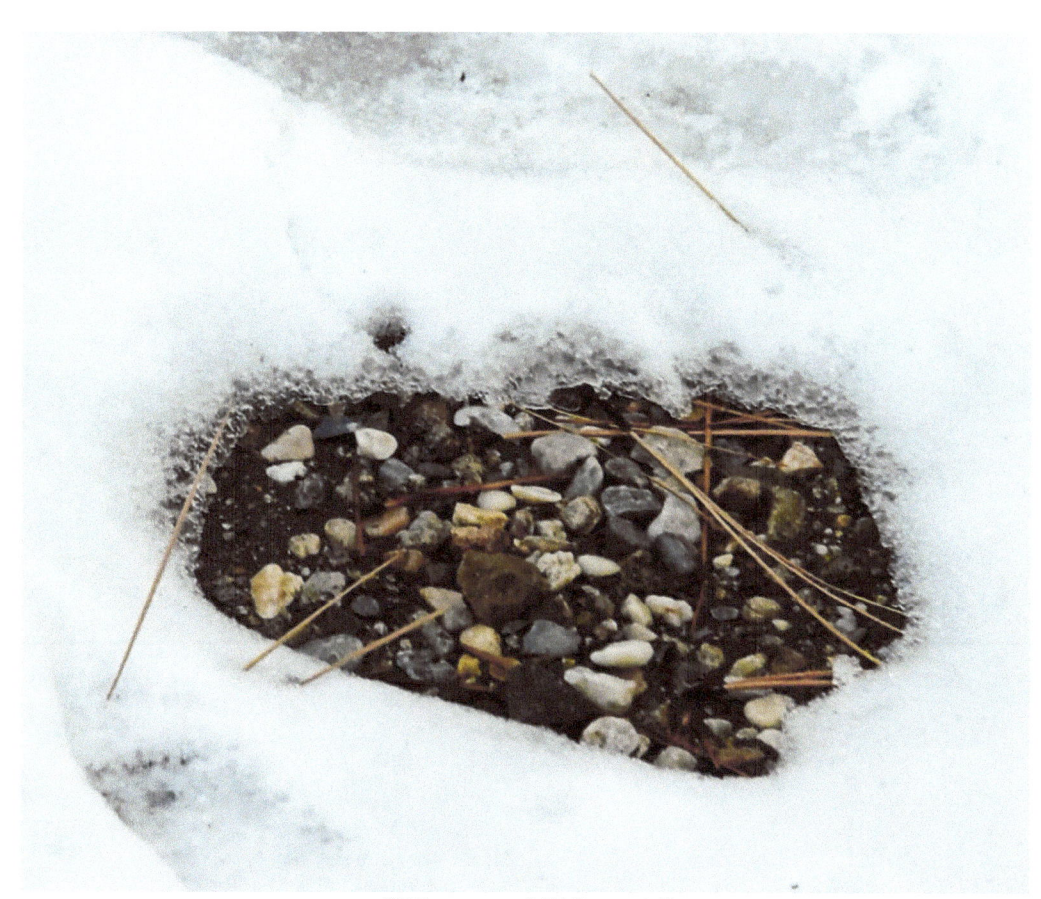

"Heart of Winter"

The weather is a friend
if you make it one.
-Jennifer Jones

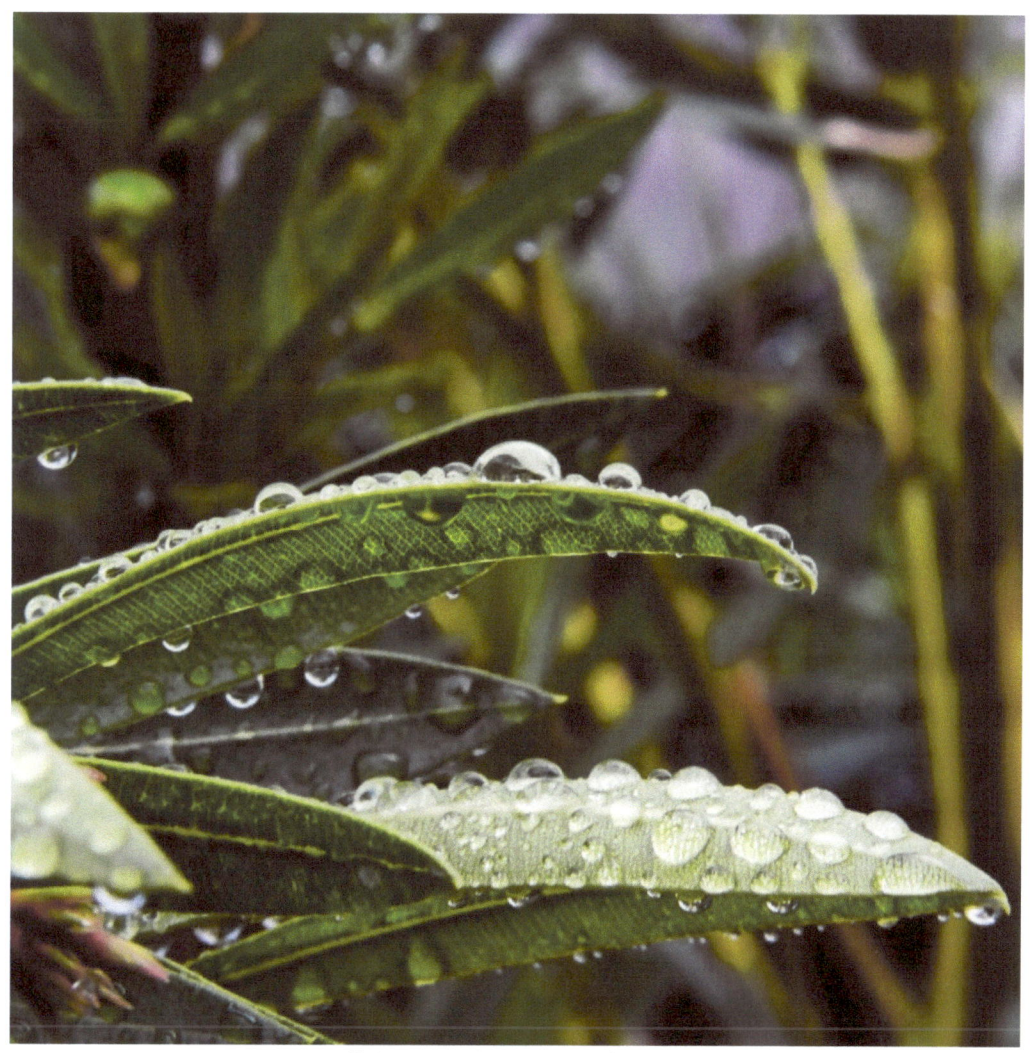

"Crystal Magnifiers"

Winter is a time of promise...
-Stanley Crawford

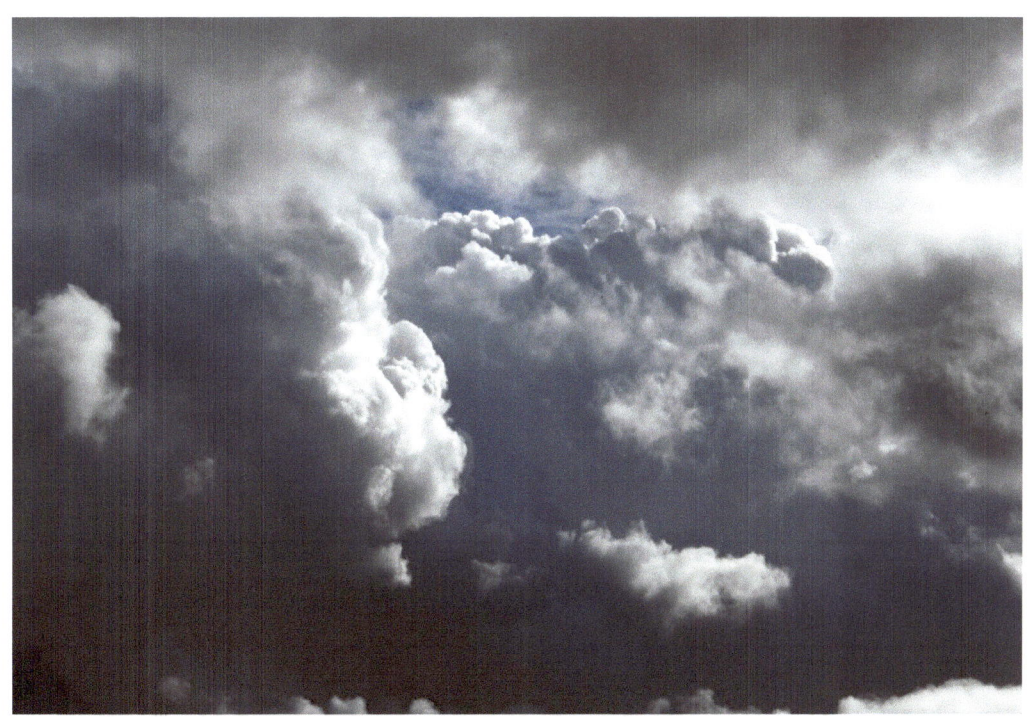

"Dark Finger of God"

The color of winter
is in the imagination.
-Terri Guillemets

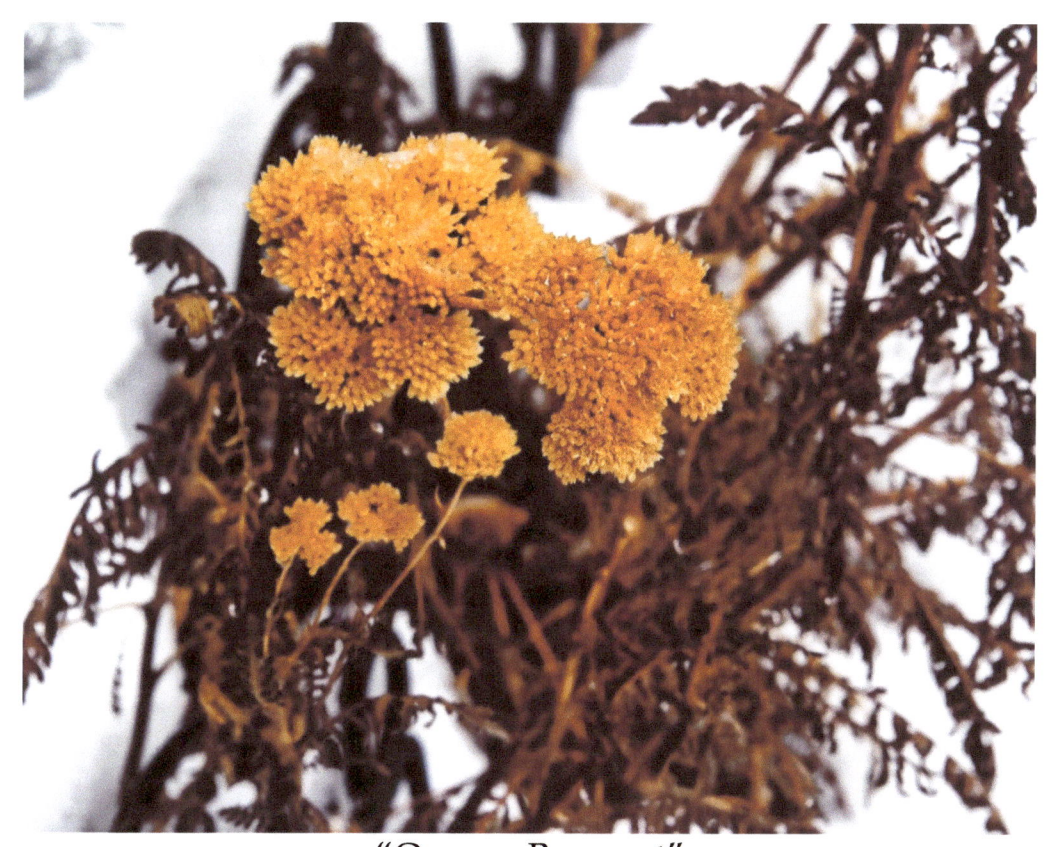

"Orange Bouquet"

One faire day in winter
makes not birds merrie.
-George Herbert

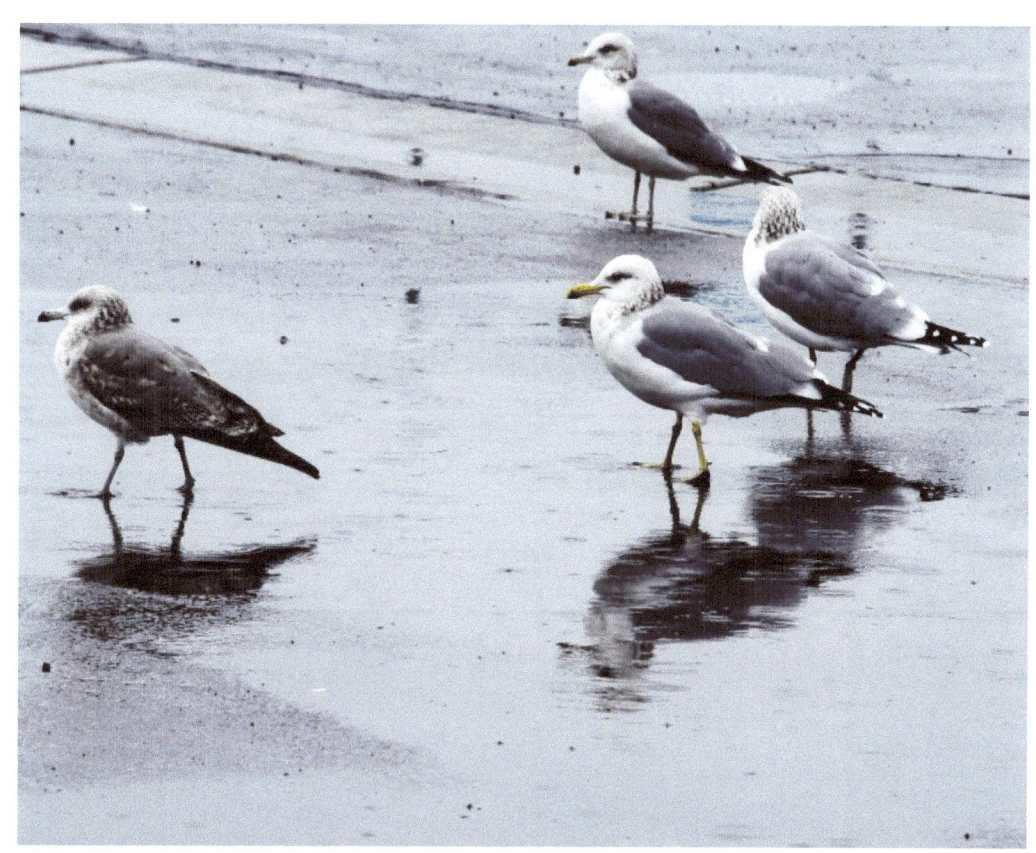

"Wet Feathers"

Welcome, winter. Your late dawns and chilled breath make me lazy, but I love you nonetheless.
-Terri Guillemets

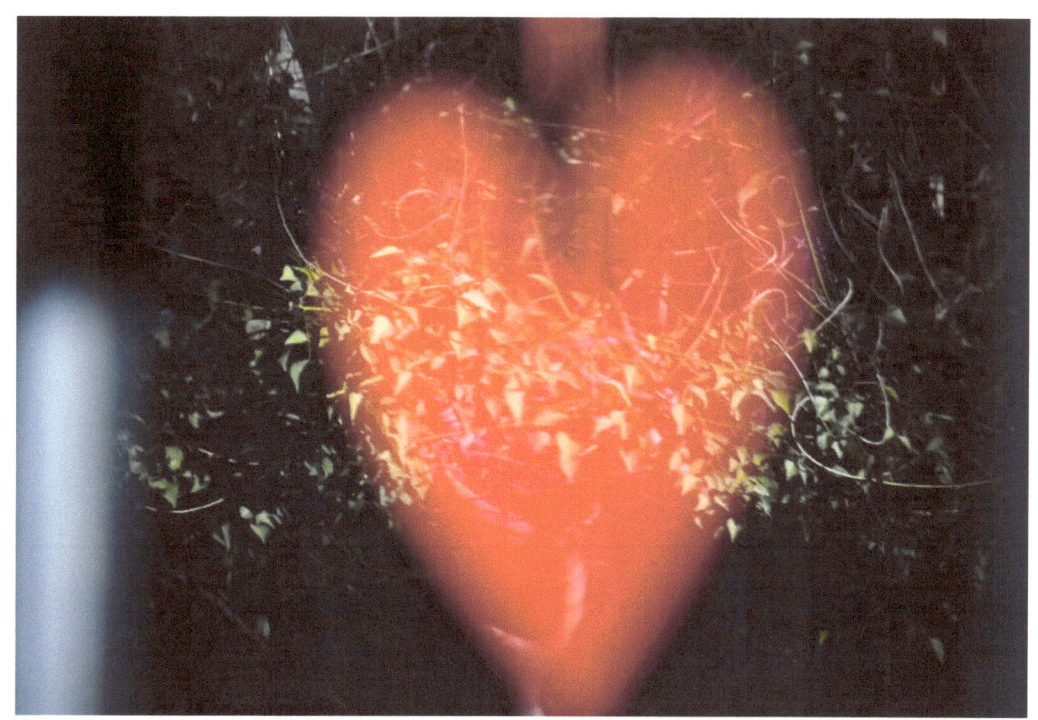

"Heart in Reflection"

There is nothing in the world more beautiful than the forest clothed to its very hollows in snow.
-William Sharp

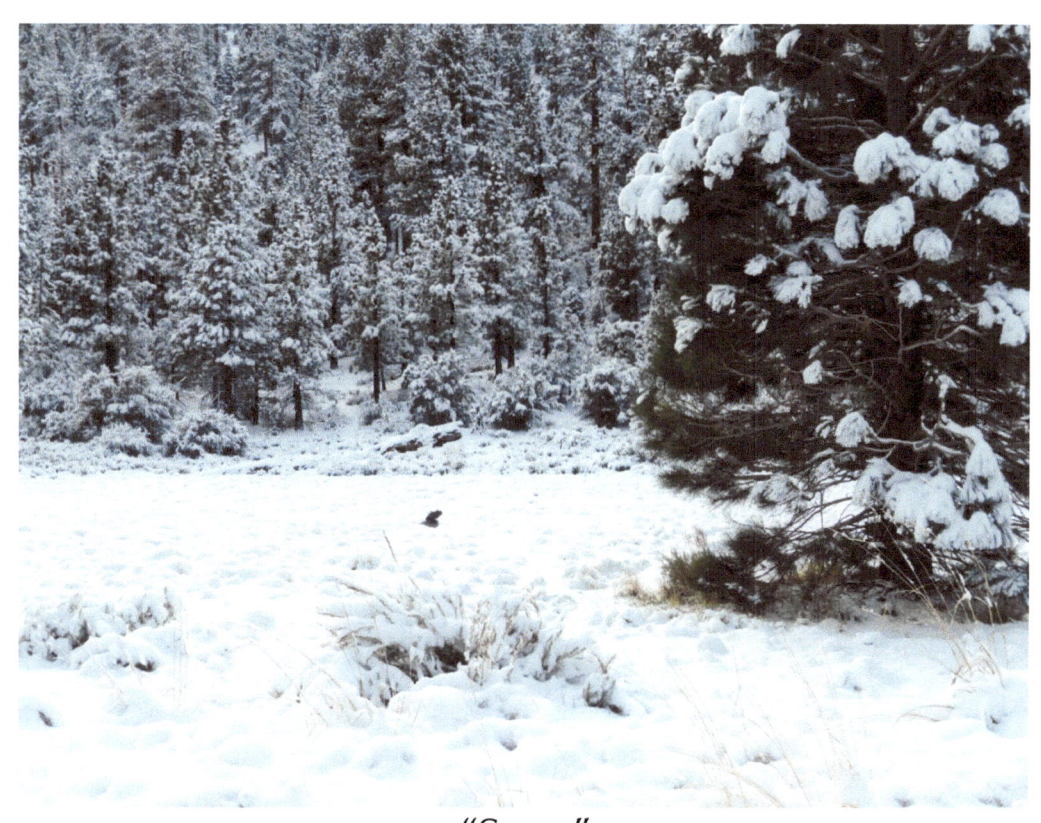

"Snow"

Winter giveth the fields,
and the trees so old,
Their beards of icicles and snow...
-Charles duc d'Orléans

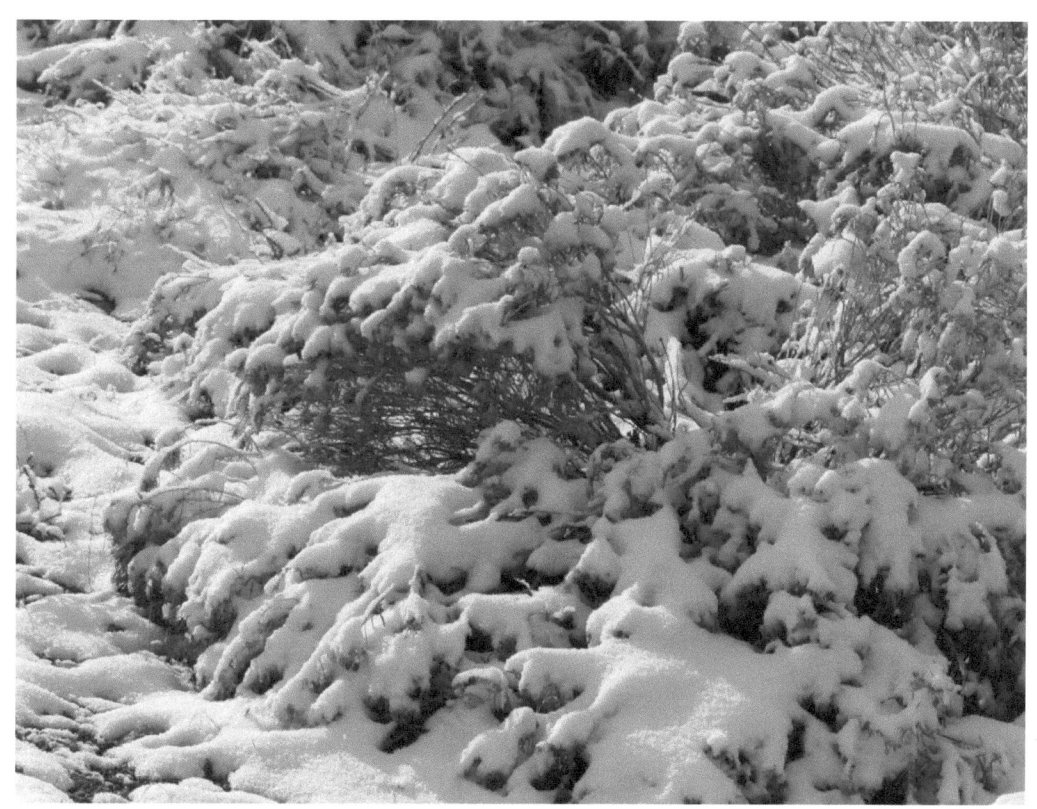

"Beard of Snow"

It is said that in a certain faraway land the cold is so intense that words freeze as soon as they are uttered, and after some time thaw and become audible, so that words spoken in winter go unheard until the next summer.

-Author Unknown

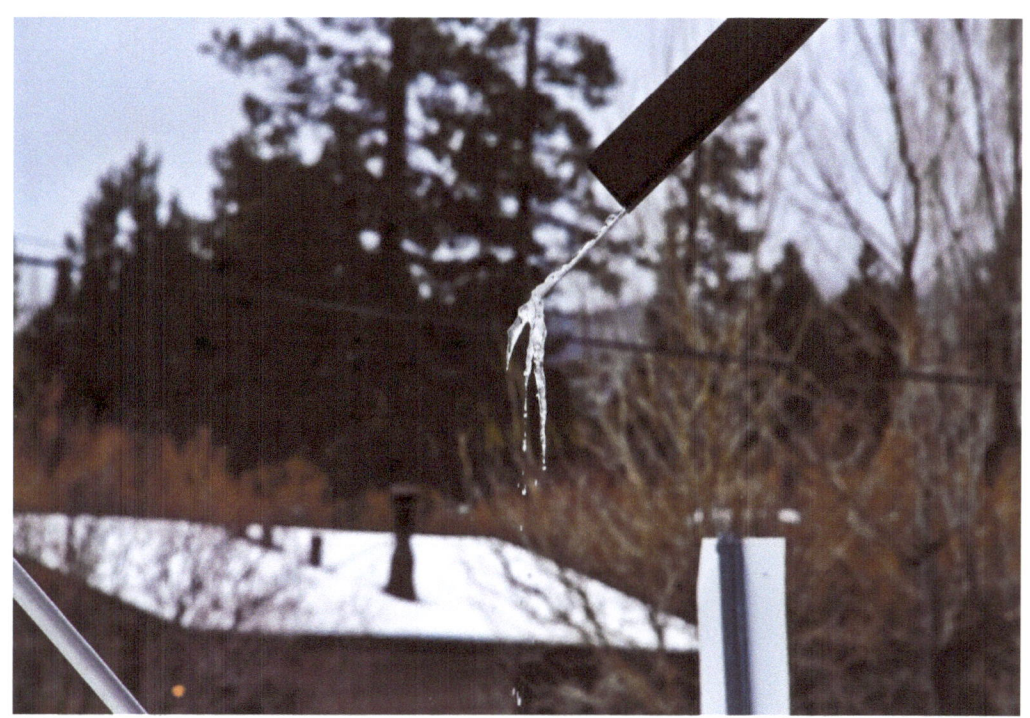

"Frozen"

My soul is full of longing for the secret of the sea, and the heart of the great ocean sends a thrilling pulse through me."
-Henry Wadsworth Longfellow

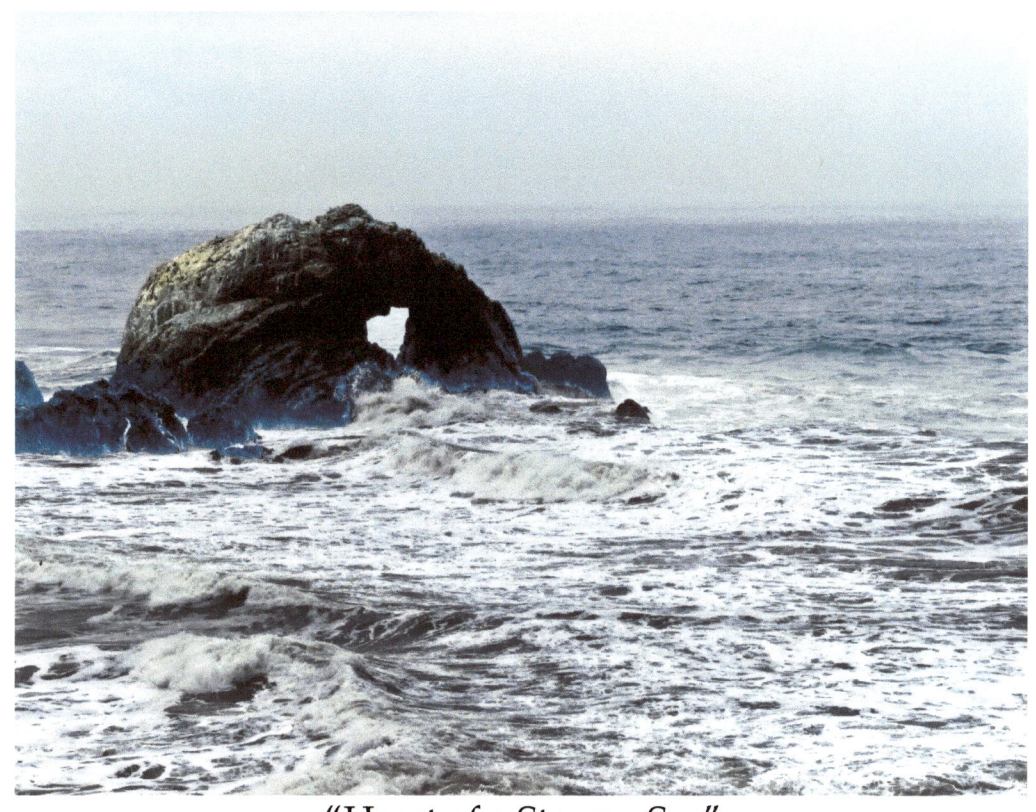

"Heart of a Stormy Sea"

What good is the warmth of summer without the cold of winter to give it sweetness?

-Author Unknown

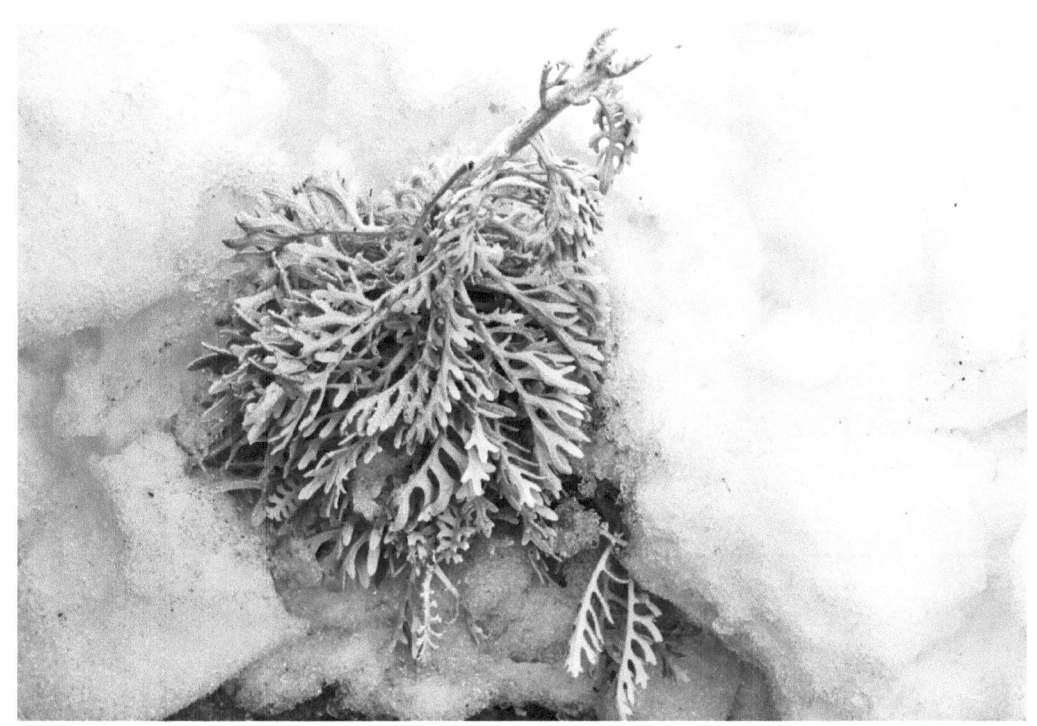

"Cold as Ice"

"I do an awful lot of thinking and dreaming about things in the past and the future - the timelessness of the rocks and the hills - all the people who have existed there. I prefer winter and fall when you feel the bone structure of the landscape - the loneliness of it, the dead feeling of winter. Something waits beneath it, the whole story doesn't show."

— *Andrew Wyeth*

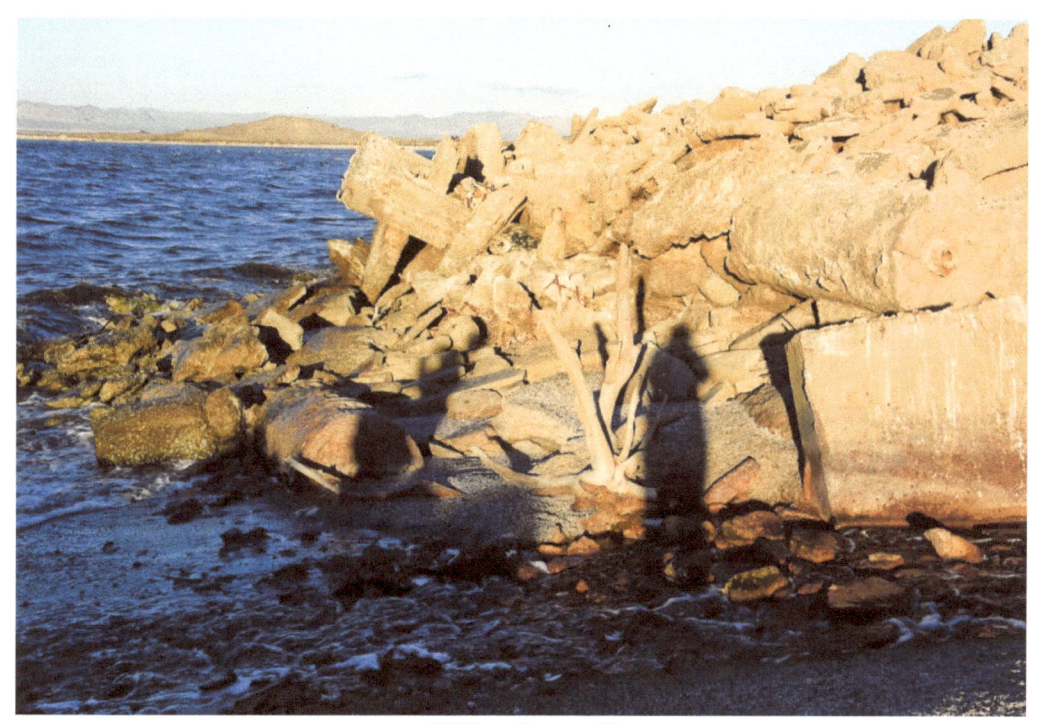

"Shadows"

"Frost grows on the window glass, forming whorl patterns of lovely translucent geometry.

— *Vera Nazarian*

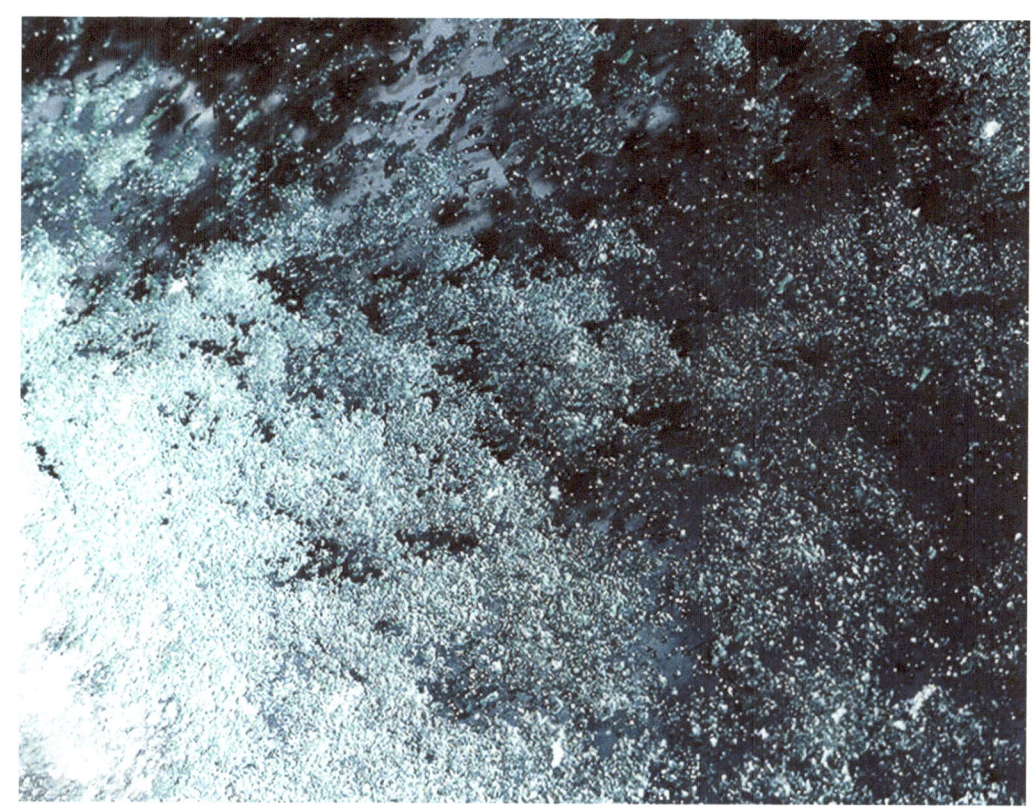

"Blue Crystals"

"Winter is a season we all wish to start and end soon."
— Karen Zirbes

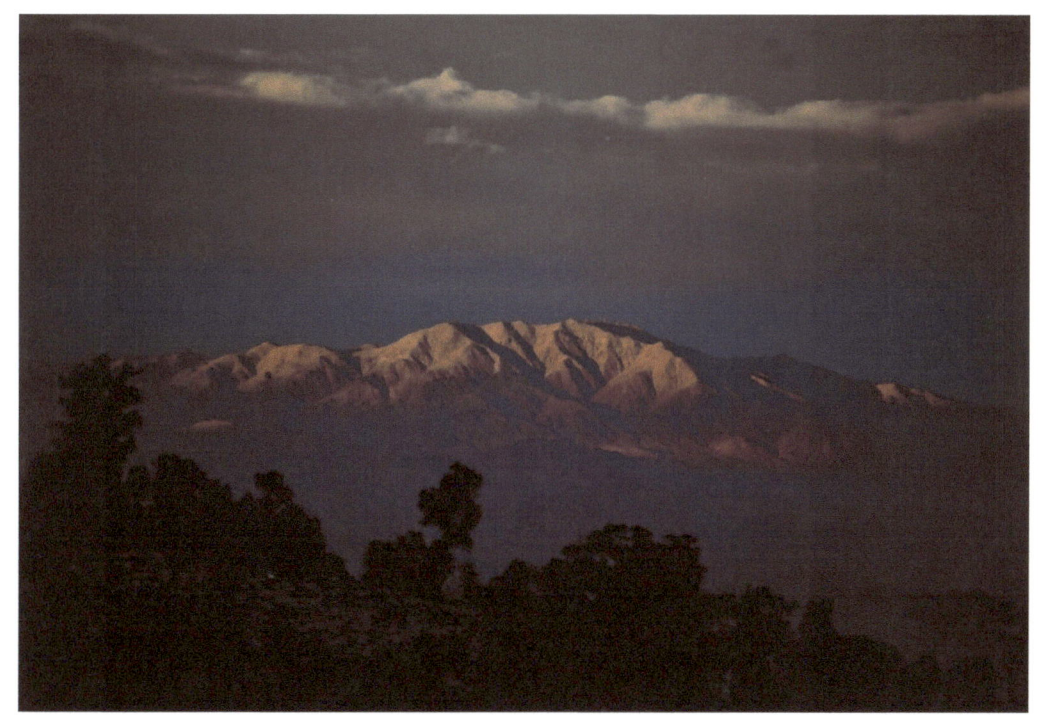

"Red Mountain Sunset"

"Winter changes into stone the water of heaven and the heart of man."
— *Victor Hugo*

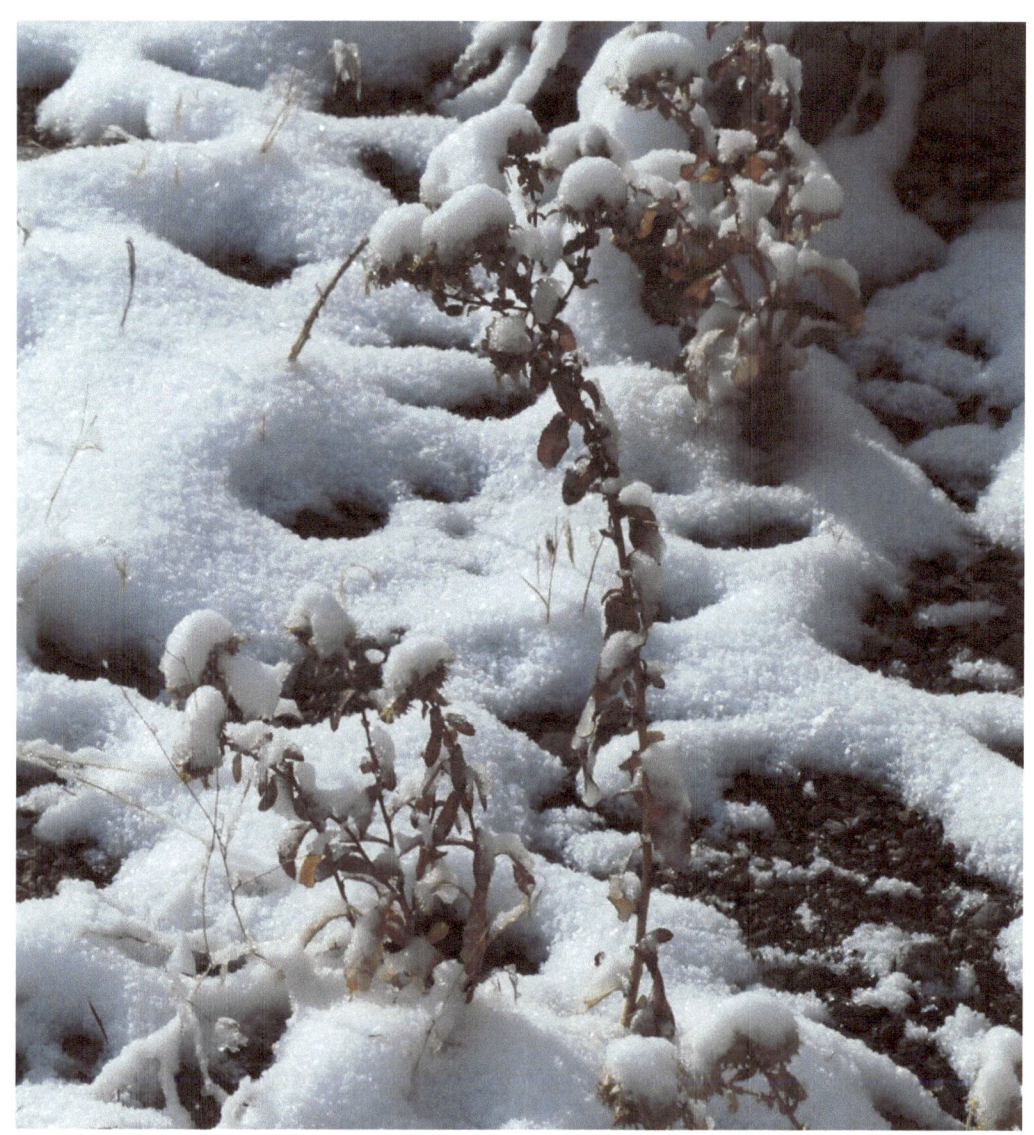

"Water Turned Stone"

*"...the winter is kind and leaves red berries
on the boughs for hungry sparrows..."*
— John Geddes

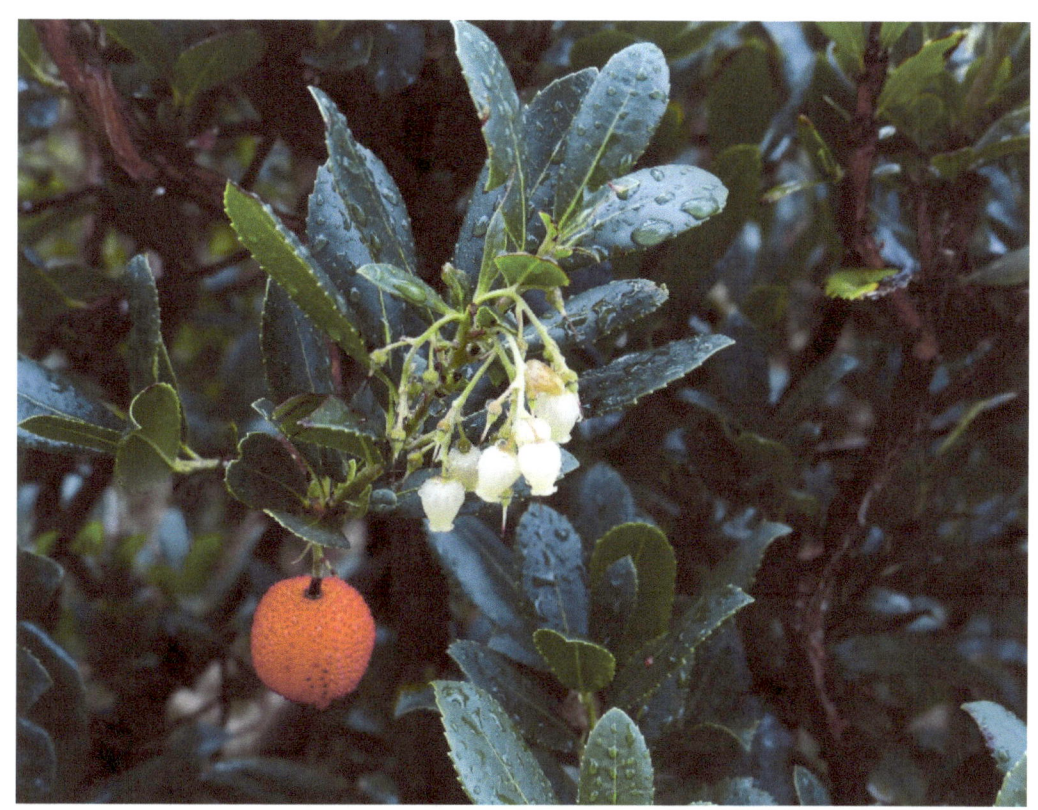

"Red Berry"

"...I pray this winter be gentle and kind - a season of rest from the wheel of the mind..."
— John Geddes

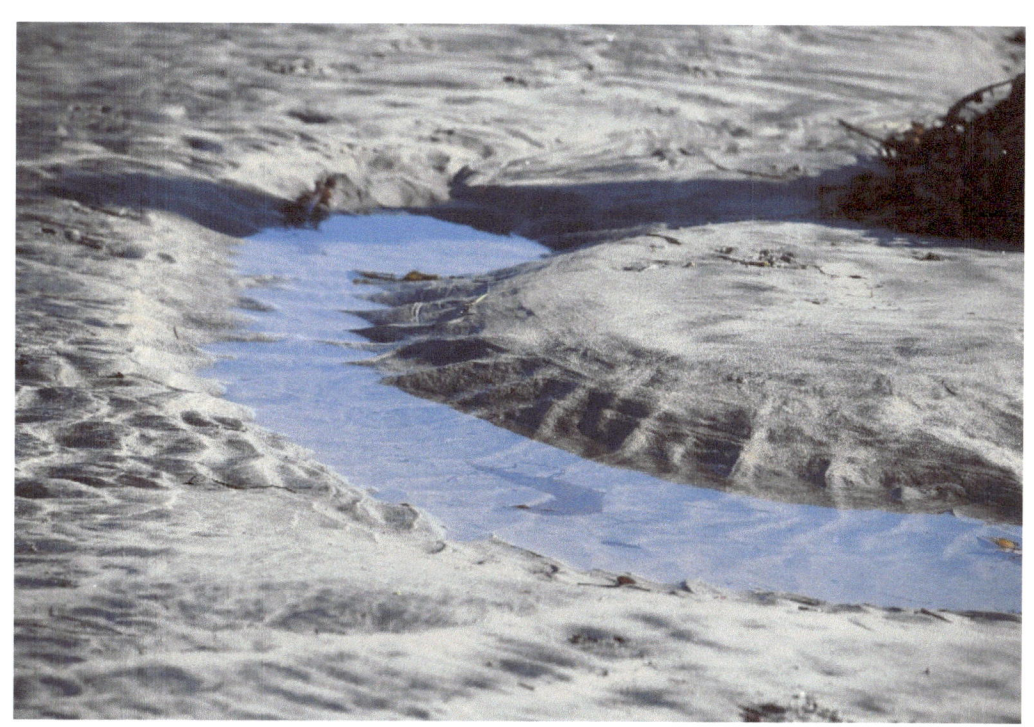

"Water Wheel"

"Now that I found you winter, I shall never forget you."
-Circe Denyer, 2015

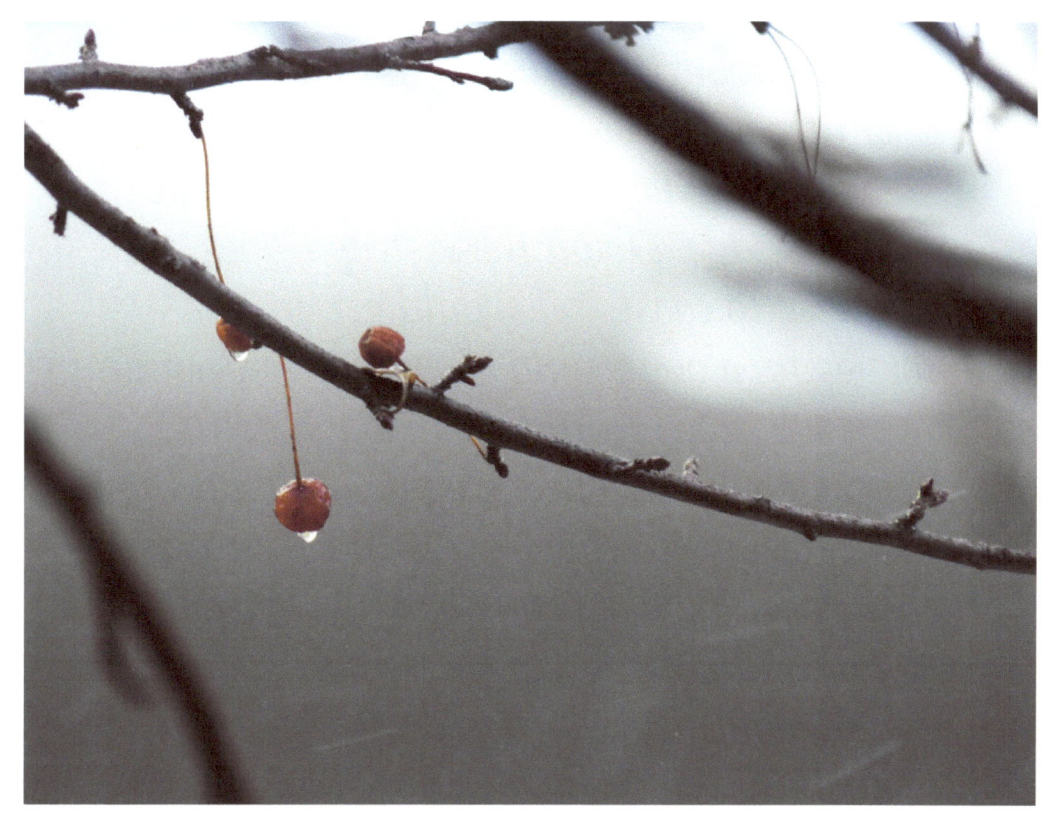

"The Rain is Done"

"Our favourite amusement during that winter was tobogganing. In places, the shore of the lake rises abruptly from the water's edge. Down these steep slopes, we used to coast. We would get on our toboggan, a boy would give us a shove, and off we went! Plunging through drifts, leaping hollows, swooping down upon the lake, we would shoot across its gleaming surface to the opposite bank. What joy! What exhilarating madness! For one wild, glad moment we snapped the chain that binds us to earth, and joining hands with the winds we felt ourselves divine!"
— *Helen Keller, The Story of My Life*

Winter

It was a season
I wished
Would never come

And then

A week of
Exploration
Friendship
Newness
Imagery

Then

Awakening to the
Breath that winter
Brings with itself
When nothing can be heard
Except the soft sounds of snow

Winter come
I wait for you
To show me something new
In your quiet season

-Circe Denyer, 2015

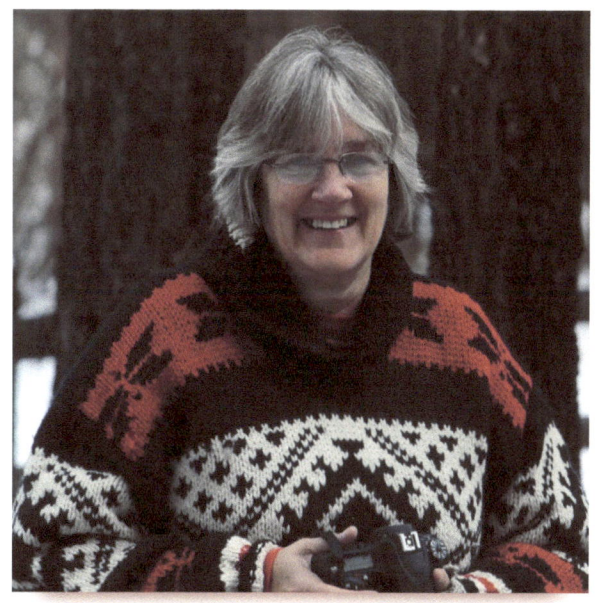

About the Photographer

Photographs were a part of the author's life since age 12. In looking back, her work has not changed from images of water, scenics, bugs, and other forms of nature. Loving the bokeh background and clear subject, blending the two.

Always looking for something unique in the images, a light, translucence, reflection, texture or pattern, each image carries with it a feeling and its own voice.

Her work is available on two stock photography sales sites, **Dreamstime** and **Public Domain Pictures**.

http://www.dreamstime.com/circed_info
http://bit.ly/circedpdplatest

See her work at http://circed.com

DEAD
OF
WINTER